NEW ZEALAND
BIRD
CALLS

LYNNETTE MOON

GEOFF MOON

JOHN KENDRICK

KAREN BAIRD

NEW
HOLLAND

Cape Reinga

HAURAKI GULF ISLANDS DETAIL

Hauturu/
Little Barrier I.

Great
Barrier I.

Bay of Islands

Hauraki
Gulf

NORTHLAND

Whangarei

Tiritiri
Matangi I.

Firth of
Thames

Hauraki
Gulf

AUCKLAND

Coromandel
Peninsula

Auckland

Miranda

North Island

WAIKATO

Tauranga

Hamilton

BAY OF PLENTY

Kawhia

Rotorua

EAST CAPE

Taupo

Gisborne

Lake
Taupo

New Zealand

New Plymouth

CENTRAL
PLATEAU

TARANAKI

Napier

Whanganui

HAWKE'S
BAY

Cape Kidnappers

MANAWATU /
WHANGANUI

Palmerston North

Cape Farewell

Kapiti
Island

WAIRARAPA

WELLINGTON

Nelson

Marlborough
Sounds

Wellington

NELSON /
TASMAN

Cook
Strait

MARLBOROUGH

Kaikoura

Greymouth

WEST COAST

Okarito

Christchurch

Banks
Peninsula

CANTERBURY

Haast

Mt Aspiring
National Park

Lake Pukaki

South Island

Lake
Wanaka

Wanaka

Oamaru

Lake
Wakatipu

Queenstown

OTAGO

FIORDLAND

Dunedin

Otago Peninsula

SOUTHLAND

Catlins Forest
Park

Invercargill

N

Rakiura/Stewart Island

CONTENTS

INSIDE BACK COVER —
CD WITH 60 BIRD CALLS

ACKNOWLEDGEMENTS

My thanks to Belinda Cooke for the opportunity to write this book, together with Johnny Kendrick's superb bird call recordings. I am particularly grateful to Matt Turner not only for editing the text, but also for his constant encouragement and advice. As always, my late husband, Geoff Moon, has been my inspiration, and the inclusion of his photographs completes a special book.

Lynnette Moon

I owe so much to my dear late wife Lorna, who had to put up with a largely absent husband on account of all those field trips, and to our three children, Shelley, Karen and Chris, who were similarly short-changed. My special thanks go to Karen for her help in assembling and editing all the bird calls that feature on the CD, and to Geoff for his good companionship over so many years.

John Kendrick (1922–2013)

THE AUTHORS

Lynnette Moon has an abiding interest in the environment. This is her third book on the subject of birds, following *The Singing Island: The story of Tiritiri Matangi* and the bestselling *Know Your New Zealand Birds* (New Holland Publishers). She has also written several school readers on natural history subjects.

Geoff Moon, OBE, Hon.FPSNZ (1915–2009) was an outstanding bird photographer with many books to his name, including *New Zealand: Land of Birds*, *A Photographic Guide to Birds of New Zealand*, and *New Zealand Forest Birds and their World* (New Holland Publishers).

Karen Baird has more than 25 years' experience in conservation. Formerly with the Department of Conservation (DOC), she currently works with the Royal Forest and Bird Protection Society, and also runs wildlife tours in New Zealand and the wider Pacific region.

In a naturalist's career spanning half a century, **John Kendrick** recorded New Zealand's birds on film and tape. The unique collection he compiled includes calls that have heralded Radio New Zealand National's *Morning Report* since 1969. In 2010, John was awarded the Queen's Service Medal and he died, aged 91 years, in 2013.

MEMOIRS OF A SOUND RECORDIST

John Kendrick (1922–2013) shares some memories of his long association with the late Geoff Moon, New Zealand's most renowned bird photographer, whose images illustrate this book.

My first trip with Geoff was in 1958. 'I'll show you some fairy terns and New Zealand dotterels at Pakiri Beach,' he said, so off we went in his Land Rover with another friend, John Warham. I shot some movie footage on my old Canon 8 mm and Geoff took photos.

I first met Geoff through mutual ornithological Society friends Ross and Betty McKenzie, having joined the society in 1955. At the time, I was running my own radio and electronics business, and Ross was keen for me to make sound recordings of his local kokako population in the Hunuas near Clevedon. In those days I had a fairly rough-and-ready valve tape recorder. We staked out a plot below an old miro tree frequented by the birds, and made the first ever sound recordings of a kokako. From then on I was hooked! My next unit I built myself as it was hard to get a decent, portable and affordable recorder in those days. It ran off car batteries, requiring an inverter, which made it less than portable. Some years later, the Wildlife Service purchased the Nagra 3, a Swiss-built professional machine, which transformed my recording quality from then on.

Geoff's skills as a veterinarian were often put to use on wild birds. I once arrived at his house to find he had patched up a morepork with a damaged wing. I believe he let it go outside their bach at Scandretts Bay, which is where he got some of his first photos of moreporks. Keenly interested in bird behaviour, he always took opportunities to help birds and learn more about them.

Quite early in our association Geoff proposed a three-week safari to photograph a recent Australian immigrant, the black-

John (left) and Geoff on Kapiti Island during filming of the Natural History Unit production Sanctuary, *part of the* Wild South series, in 1988.

fronted dotterel, which was now to be found in the riverbeds of the Hawke's Bay and central North Island. Geoff's friend Clive Wickens owned a magnificent Ford station-wagon. After much planning, we set off south in the spring of 1961, the Ford crammed to the gunwales with kit. En route, we visited the Kaimanawas, where we tramped for two hours up the Waipakihi River and found a great many riflemen – and a rifleman nest. Geoff was keen to go back to the car for a hide, adding four hours to our walk, but I assured him we would find another rifleman's nest on our three-week tour. (Sadly, we never did, and Geoff would periodically remind me of this great loss.) Anyway, off to the Hawke's Bay, where we walked up and down the Tukituki, Ngaruroro and Tutaekuri rivers. We eventually found nests of the black-fronted dotterel and set up hides.

To be good at photographing from hides you have to know birds and their behaviour,

and Geoff generously shared all his secrets and skills. When I joined the Wildlife Service, these skills assisted me a great deal. He taught me, for instance, how to set up a hide without disturbing the birds. (As he was always careful to point out, the birds' welfare took priority over any photography.) The trick was to move it bit by bit into position, so that the bird gradually got used to it.

After this, we went on many an expedition together. There were voyages on the launch of Gordon McKenzie, a Clevedon friend, to photograph spotted shags diving for fish at the northern cliffs of Waiheke Island, and up through the islands off the Coromandel coast, taking in the gannet colony at Happy Jack Island/Motukahaua. On another trip, Geoff and I went with Len Doel to the South Island for the cirl buntings. It was a little early for nesting, but I did get the first recordings of cirl buntings and Geoff some pictures.

I had sold my business in 1963 and applied for a position as an audio-visual officer with the Wildlife Service, transferring to Wellington in 1964. Luckily, Geoff was appointed to the Veterinary Council, whose meetings were held in Wellington, which meant he could

John in the field in the 1970s: watching birds (above) and recording (left).

sit me at my home in York Bay. There was
ways an opportunity to do something
rnithological when he came down.

In January 1964, the Wildlife Service felt
e knew enough about saddlebacks on Hen
land, so they sent us out to catch thirty birds
d move them to Middle Chicken. Geoff
as invited to come along to photograph
d provide veterinary advice. I had already
otained a number of recordings of the birds
August and September 1963, but I took
e recording gear, as I realised it could make
l the difference in capturing the birds.
on Merton brought the first mist nets, which
e set up in suitable places, then I planted
y speakers one each side of the mist net.
sing my sound recordings, and a rather
attered-looking saddleback decoy – a new
chnique in those days – we lured the birds
to the net, switching the sound from one
eaker to the other to draw them in. Every
orning, each of us gathered half a jar of
sects and grubs to feed the birds. Once we
d collected our thirty, the birds were crated,
e Navy picked us up and we took them to
iddle Chicken – the first successful release
saddlebacks anywhere.

Later, we were both involved in the early
akapo searches at Esperance Valley in
ordland in 1973, working with Don Merton
d others. Good-quality recordings were
sential to enable us to capture the birds.
eoff's role was critical, too: to look after the
elfare of captive birds and see them safely
their new home of Maud Island. (One of
em, which we had christened Richard Henry
ter an early naturalist, survived until 2010.)
After I had retired from the Wildlife Service
1982, we visited Kapiti together. We had

been watching kaka, but it's hard to find the
nests of these secretive birds. I eventually saw
one acting suspiciously, and sure enough, we
found a nest inside a tree trunk with several
different holes. We set up a hide and spent
many hours happily observing and recording
their behaviour. There was a return to Kapiti
in 1988, when Mike Hacking, a director
for the Natural History Unit, made a film
about my sound recording work and Geoff's
photography and set it on the island. The
documentary, titled *Sanctuary*, was part of
the *Wild South* series and included some of
my own film material, as well as some great
shots of Geoff's hide work.

Geoff and I continued to do many birding
excursions in our retirement until ill health
prevented him from getting out in the field. I
remember Geoff as a generous mentor, whose
deep fund of knowledge was shared with
many people, and as a skilful photographer
and wonderful friend.

eoff shooting New Zealand falcon nests in the 1990s.

INTRODUCTION

Listening out for birds

Birds may call for a variety of reasons: for example, to announce or reinforce a claim to their territory, or to attract a mate. They tend to remain in areas where they can find food, so it helps if you know, for instance, that some forest birds feed high up in the forest. The kaka often feeds in the canopy, and although it may at first be hard to spot, its harsh calls will reveal its presence. Likewise birds that feed near water tend to spend more time there.

Dawn is a special time to listen to birds, whether in a garden or a forest, as many of the birds sing together in a 'dawn chorus', though you may at first be unlikely to pick ou individual songs.

Some species don't make obvious calls; many of the finches, for instance, make similar-sounding chattering calls. Others call when on the wing. Examples of these include the white-faced heron, which utters loud croaks in flight, and the incessant *kek-kek-ke* of Cook's petrel, heard particularly on damp nights as it flies low overhead.

Birdsong also varies through the year. Liste out in spring when the calls of many birds are more prominent. You will soon come to know the whistling calls of the shining cucko (back from its winter quarters in the Solomo

Above: A kokako singing at dawn.
Right: The white-faced heron gives a distinctive croak.

ve: The morepork's name is a rendition of the bird's call.

ands) and the loud call of the New Zealand
ngfisher. Even if they cannot be seen, you
n at least be sure these birds are nearby.

earning from birds' calls

l birds make sounds unique to them
lthough differences can be subtle, and one
two species, such as the starling, are able
imitate other birds). Additionally, each
rd makes a range of sounds, according to
hether it is alarmed, making display calls to
mate, or simply keeping in touch with that
ate while feeding. Once you get to know
e alarm call of the blackbird, look around:
ou may well spot the intruder – a prowling
t, for instance, or another predator – that is
itating the bird. Chicks, too, call particularly
udly, with excited cheeping, when they hear
parent approach or when being fed.

TIPS ON LISTENING TO BIRD CALLS

- Focus on just one or two birds to begin
with in order to familiarise yourself
gradually with each species and its calls.
- Sit quietly when listening, as movement
or voices may scare birds away and muffle
quieter calls.
- Take a notebook so you can record your
impressions of calls and bird behaviour, as
well as notes on the conditions (weather,
season, time of day, temperature, etc.)
- Take extra care when birds are nesting
in spring. It is never a good idea to
play the recorded calls outside as birds
may become alarmed, and if breeding,
they might even desert their nest. As an
alternative, you may wish to record the
CD onto a pocket listening device fitted
with earphones.

HOW TO USE THIS BOOK

• The text provides basic information about each bird, such as its plumage or behaviour, or its distribution and preferred habitat. You will also find notes on what the bird eats and where it nests. The running order of the 60 species follows the *Checklist of the Birds of New Zealand* (Ornithological Society of New Zealand with Te Papa Press, fourth edition, 2010).

• Each entry in the book is supported by a track on the CD containing the bird's call or song. Track numbers correspond to the entry numbers in the book. In some cases, each track is made up of more than one separate call. For instance, Track 41 (Blackbird) begins with the male's territorial song and concludes with the alarm call.

Entry number, common name and (where applicable) Maori name of bird.

Text contains information about distribution, habitat, plumage and behaviour.

Look out for the icons that indicate food and nesting information.

Information about the call and the corresponding track number on the CD can be found at the bottom of each page.

24 | New Zealand Dotterel
Tuturiwhatu

This threatened dotterel is now mainly seen north of Hawke's Bay and Kawhia, apart from a small population on Stewart Island (which is a separate subspecies). The bird is often heard before it is seen because it is so well camouflaged on sandy beaches, its pale brown-and-white winter plumage changing to a sandy russet prior to breeding. The dotterel walks or runs rapidly, and bobs its head distinctively when pausing to feed.

 Takes molluscs and crustaceans (such as sandhoppers) from sand, crabs from mud, and crickets and worms from grass.

 A scrape in the sand is often placed near driftwood or clumps of marram grass or spinifex. On Stewart Island, nests inland in low vegetation on the open tops.

 TRACK N° 24

Calls commonly a series of short *churps*, a single *prip*, reedy *trrrt* and *turr* sounds, or when disturbed, a high-pitched, explosive *pweep* or *chip*.

25 | Spur-winged Plover

The spur-winged plover or masked lapwing is about the size of a rock pigeon, with grey-brown upper parts, white underparts, black head and nape, and yellow bill and wattles. The yellow spur on the shoulder of each wing may be used defensively or in display. Now common throughout New Zealand, the plover occurs on pastures, riverbeds, lagoons, lake shores and sheltered coasts. It flies with a distinctive floppy wingbeat. Birds are often seen in pairs; flocks may form in autumn.

 Crustaceans and molluscs on coast; insects and worms on pastureland.

 Usually a depression in pasture or on shingle, lined with a few strands of grass. In arable pasture pairs may nest on buildings.

 TRACK N° 25

Noisy, rattling and rather grating call of *kitter-kitter-kitter* or *rikka-rikka*. Utters loud staccato sounds at night.

Brown Kiwi

Immature brown kiwi (left); young chick brooded by male (above).

…sily our most famous bird, the kiwi is also …e of the least visible, although it may be …ard calling at night.

Of the five kiwi species, the North Island …own kiwi is the best-known, inhabiting …rest and scrub over a widespread but …calised distribution. In the South Island, …own kiwi comprise two species: the rowi, …which there is a small colony in Okarito … the West Coast, and the tokoeka, which …habits the Haast and Fiordland areas as well …Stewart Island. (The other two kiwi species …e the great spotted kiwi or roroa, found in …me upland parts of the South Island, and …e little spotted kiwi, now confined to a few …ands and mainland sanctuaries.)

Entirely flightless, kiwi are the smallest …embers of an ancient family that included …e now-extinct moa. There is no tail, the …ings are tiny and the eyes small, and the …umage consists of thick, bristly feathers. …e senses of smell and hearing are acute, …abling kiwi to locate food at night below …e surface of the soil and among leaf litter. …ostrils are located near the bill tip, which …ntains additional sensory organs that detect

vibrations of prey moving in the soil. Large, muscular legs and strong feet allow kiwi to run swiftly and kick strongly when attacked.

Predation by ferrets, stoats and dogs threatens kiwi populations nationally.

 The kiwi feeds at night by probing its long bill into the ground to capture worms and grubs. It also takes fallen fruit, as well as insects from among leaf litter.

 Nest locations include burrows in the ground, cavities among tree roots, hollow logs, depressions in stream banks and thickets of dense vegetation.

TRACK N° 01

Territorial calls of North Island brown kiwi are (male) a high whistle and (female) a deep, rasping call: calls of both sexes rise in a *ki–wii* sound. Snuffles noisily while feeding.

11

2 | Black Swan

First introduced from Australia in the 1860s, the black swan has thrived in New Zealand and is today widespread on urban lakes, lagoons and estuaries. It is easily identified by the overall black plumage. The wings have large white tips, which are visible when spread (as in flight). Birds may nest in a colony or as a single pair, and are aggressive when defending their nests. During the autumn moult, black swans congregate on secluded lakes for safety.

 Leaves and shoots of aquatic plants; eelgrass in estuaries. Birds also go ashore to graze on pastures.

 The large nest, built of reeds and vegetation and lined with feathers, is usually situated near the water's edge.

TRACK N° **02**

Musical bugles and hoarse honking calls carry far on the water and in flight, especially at night. Also utters whistles and, when threatened, loud hisses.

3 | Paradise Shelduck
Putangitangi

Found throughout New Zealand, paradise shelduck favour open spaces, such as the big riverbeds in the South Island high country, or grazed pastureland elsewhere.

Usually seen in pairs, these large birds are easy to identify, with the female's white head and deep chestnut body and the male's overall dark plumage. Pairs occupy and defend a territory most of the year, although they will form flocks on small lakes during the late summer moulting period.

 Grasses, clover, grain and aquatic vegetation.

 A nest made of grasses and lined with down is built in a rock crevice, hollow log, clump of tussock or even high up in a large tree hole.

TRACK N° **03**

Calls are often duets. Female gives a high-pitched *zeek-zeek*; male utters a deep *honk-honk* if disturbed. In flocks, birds trumpet discordantly and utter guttural *glink-glink* calls.

Blue Duck
Whio

e rare blue duck lives in turbulent, bush-
nged rivers of both main islands, in alpine
eas and at lower altitudes. It is scarce north
the central plateau. Superbly suited to this
abitat, it can swim and dive rapidly in swift
rrents. Secretive by nature, the blue duck is
sily overlooked, its blue-grey plumage well
mouflaged among boulders. In flight, the
rd's wingbeat is rapid and its course direct.
rds are usually seen in pairs and are very
efensive of their territory.

 Feeding at dusk and dawn, it dives for
invertebrates such as caddis-fly larvae,
and also takes insects on the surface.

 The nest of foliage and sticks is lined
with grasses and feathers and sited in a
cavity or thicket on the riverbank.

 TRACK N° **04**

Male calls in a high-pitched
whistling *wseow wseow*; female makes low,
rasping rattles, for example when disturbed.

5 | Brown Teal
Pateke

Brown teal were once common in wetlands
and estuaries, but is now endangered as a
result of predation by cats and stoats and the
clearance of bankside vegetation. It is still
found on Great Barrier Island and in some
estuaries on the Northland east coast. When
disturbed, flocks readily swim away rather
than fly. Breeding males sport a brown breast
and greenish head; in both sexes a white ring
circles the eye.

 Feeding mainly at dusk and dawn,
the brown teal eats a wide range of
terrestrial, freshwater and marine
invertebrates. Also grazes on pastures
at night.

 A bowl of grasses, lined with down, is
sited in thick vegetation near the water.

 TRACK N° **05**

Generally silent, but male calls with
a hoarse rasp and high-pitched piping sound;
female call is a low, repeated *quark quark*.

6 | Mallard

Introduced to New Zealand in the 1860s, the mallard is now abundant and widespread in a range of wetlands, from ponds in urban parks to shallow lagoons, rivers and estuaries. The male is colourful with an iridescent green head, yellow bill and chestnut breast, while the female's brown-flecked plumage is dull by comparison. In the hunting season, mallard take refuge with other waterfowl on lakes.

 Mainly eats aquatic vegetation. Dabbles at the water's edge for plants and seeds; upends in shallow waterways for aquatic insects and snails. On dry land, grazes on clover, seeds and grain.

 Nest is a bowl of grass, lined with down and concealed in vegetation or under trees close to the water's edge.

TRACK N° **06**

Male calls in quiet whistles and soft *quacks*, while female calls in a more vocal and harsh, repeated *quack-quack-quack*.

7 | New Zealand Scaup
Papango

The scaup is a small, squat duck favouring deep, clear freshwater lakes, including alpine lakes and lagoons throughout the country, where it usually keeps with others in small flocks. The male's plumage is a glossy black-brown and his eyes are bright yellow. The female is dull brown, with brown eyes. The scaup flies low and rapidly over water, revealing white bands in the flight feathers.

 Feeds more actively at dawn and dusk, diving deeply for aquatic insects, fish, tadpoles and the shoots of water plants.

 A bowl of reeds and grasses, lined with feathers, is located near the water's edge. Pairs often nest in close proximity.

TRACK N° **07**

General calls are soft, musical chittering sounds. Male calls with muted whistles; female utters low quacks. In courtship, birds call in soft, wheezy whistles and a *whee-whee*.

Yellow-eyed Penguin
Hoiho

e endemic yellow-eyed penguin is one
 the world's rarest penguins. It inhabits
 south-eastern coast of the South Island,
 well as Rakiura/Stewart Island and the
 bantarctic Islands. Like all penguins, it is
ghtless, with sleek, narrow and waterproof
athers, and flat wings modified into flippers.
 land, the bird stands upright, though it
timid and wary of predators, such as dogs.
hen coming ashore to breed or to moult, it
alks with a shuffling gait.

9 | Blue Penguin
Korora

The world's smallest penguin, the blue or
little penguin is commonly seen on the coasts
of New Zealand and the Chatham Islands. The
small, compact feathers are a metallic blue-
grey, and the breast and undersides of the
flippers are white. The penguin is usually seen
singly or in small groups. It swims rapidly and
may be seen floating on the water, resting on
its side, between dives. After fishing all day,
and usually after dark, it comes ashore and
scurries to its roost or nest site.

 Catches squid, fish and krill in its razor-
sharp bill.

 A flattened scrape lined with grasses is
well hidden among coastal scrub or flax
or against logs. Nest area is often used
year-round as a roost.

 Feeds near the shore, usually close to
the surface, taking small fish and squid.

 Nests are simple scrapes hidden in
rock crevices, caves and burrows, and
sometimes beneath seaside dwellings.

TRACK N° 08

Mates exchange trumpetings and
piercing trills as one approaches the roost to take
over incubation. Birds also utter a kiwi-like call,
and a shrill barking in full cry, becoming vibrato.

TRACK N° 09

Very noisy when coming ashore at
night to roost, uttering moans and subdued
quacks. At nest, gives cat-like mews, screams,
wails, moans and low-toned growls.

10 | Cook's Petrel

One of the smallest of the gadfly petrels, the Cook's petrel breeds only in New Zealand: mainly on Hauturu/Little Barrier Island, with some on Great Barrier and Codfish islands. It is common in the outer Hauraki Gulf during summer. After breeding, it migrates to the eastern Pacific. The plumage is pale grey on the crown and upper wings and white on the cheeks and underparts. Most petrels have an acute sense of smell, enabling them to locate food and nest sites in the dark.

 Feeds at sea at night on crustaceans, squid and small fish. Tends to surface-feed, grabbing prey in its hooked bill.

 Digs a nesting burrow in soft soil on high, forested ridges.

11 | Australasian Gannet
Takapu

Common around our coasts, this large seabird is distinguished by snow-white plumage, a golden-yellow cap, and wide wings tipped and fringed with black. From a height of 20–30 metres the bird plunges steeply, with wings tightly folded, to catch prey. It also sweeps and glides over the surface, and flocks sometimes form over shoals of fish. Birds then make quick, low dives after fish.

 Seizes small fish, anchovies and squid in its strong serrated bill and swallows them after bobbing to the surface.

 Gannets nest together in large colonies with well-known examples at Farewell Spit, Cape Kidnappers and Muriwai. Seaweed and grasses are cemented with dirt and excreta into a mounded nest.

2 | Pied Shag
Karuhiruhi

...amed after its white throat and underparts, ...onze-black uppers and black webbed feet, ...e pied shag is the second-largest of New ...aland's 18 shag (or cormorant) species. ...und mostly in the North Island, but also in ...e Marlborough Sounds and further south, ...favours sheltered coastal waters and some ...eshwater lakes and lagoons. It may often be ...en with its wings outspread to dry.

 Catches fish, especially eels in lakes and flounder in coastal shallows. At sea, usually fishes alone and may remain submerged for 20–40 seconds.

 Colonial nester in large shoreline trees overhanging water. The bulky platform of sticks and seaweed, lined with leaves and sited in a fork, is reused annually.

 TRACK N° 12

Silent except when nesting. As adult flies to the nest and greets its mate, they call in guttural croaks, gurgling sounds and squeals; chicks solicit food with monotonous wheezy calls.

13 | White Heron
Kotuku

Largest of the heron species, this conspicuous bird is solitary in habit, and although widespread in New Zealand, it is uncommon. Favoured habitats are lagoons, marshland, lakes, rivers and tidal streams. Seen in flight, the wingbeat is leisurely, with neck held back and long black legs trailing. The breeding plumage from September onwards features long, silky back plumes and a change of bill colour from yellow to black.

 Stalks prey in shallows, raking up mud with feet. Catches invertebrates, fish, frogs, birds and small mammals with a rapid strike from the dagger-like bill.

 Nests of sticks, twigs and fern fronds are built in trees overhanging the Waitangiroto River in Okarito, Westland.

TRACK N° 13

Silent except when nesting. Pairs give loud, frog-like croaks and groans when arriving at the nest, with chicks making *clickety-click* soliciting calls.

17

14 | White-faced Heron

15 | Australasian Harrier
Kahu

An Australian species that self-introduced in the 1950s, the white-faced heron has become a common sight throughout New Zealand. It is found in a variety of wetland habitats from sheltered coasts, estuaries, harbours, lakes and marshes to open pastures and parks. The plumage is grey with a white face, and the flight features a leisurely wingbeat with neck folded and legs outstretched.

Sometimes referred to as a hawk, the Australasian or swamp harrier is common throughout New Zealand. Often seen soaring above pasture, alternately gliding and slowly flapping, it also frequents forest margins and wetlands, and may be spotted near roadsides as it investigates carrion on the tarseal. The plumage colour can indicate age: dark brown on juveniles, fading to buff on adults.

 Stalks prey carefully, or stirs it up by raking feet through tidal pools. Aquatic prey includes small fish, frogs, insects, molluscs and crustaceans; damp parkland yields earthworms, and farmland is a summer source of insects.

 Live prey includes small birds, rabbits, rodents and insects, as well as fish and tadpoles caught by wading in shallow water. Carrion is scavenged from roads.

 A large nest of loose sticks is built in a tall pine, macrocarpa or pohutukawa.

 An untidy nest of rushes, sticks and grasses, lined with feathers, is placed on the ground among raupo, scrub or fern. Harriers are secretive when nesting.

TRACK N° 14

Plaintive *kark* or guttural *graaw* in flight, also heard when alighting at the nest, when it ends with a repeated *gow-gow-gow*. Alarm call is a high-pitched *wrank*.

TRACK N° 15

Usually silent, but when courting birds perform aerial displays they call in a squealing *kee-kee* and *kee-o*, with a repeated whistle. Also make mewing sounds, especially at nest.

A juvenile (left) lacks the adult's yellow cere and eye rim; chicks (above) are fed torn pieces of prey.

6 | New Zealand Falcon
Karearea

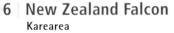

[N]ew Zealand's sole resident falcon species is [cl]assified in three races according to habitat. [Th]e eastern falcon inhabits the South Island [hi]gh country, the southern falcon occupies [Fi]ordland and Stewart Island, and the bush [fal]con occurs in the North Island and the [no]rth-west of the South Island.

The New Zealand falcon is immediately [di]stinguishable from the Australasian harrier, [be]ing a little over half the size, with short, [ro]unded wings, a long tail, and a swift, [di]rect flight. The wing shape helps the falcon [m]anoeuvre through forest and so exploit this [sp]ecialised habitat as a source of prey.

Like many raptors, the falcon possesses [ac]ute eyesight, which is much more sensitive [th]an that of humans. Unlike the harrier, the [fal]con takes only live prey, captured in high-[di]ving swoops at up to 200 km/h, and also [du]ring fast flight just above ground level. [Br]eeding pairs keep large territories [an]d are fearless in defence of their nest sites.

The ground nests are vulnerable to [in]troduced predators such as stoats, cats and [do]gs, and the species is listed today as near-threatened. Falcons have established territories in Kaingaroa Forest in the central North Island, where an abundance of prey in the form of small birds has aided successful breeding.

One of New Zealand's foremost centres for raptor research and conservation is the Wingspan Birds of Prey Trust at Rotorua, where visitors can see falcons in flying demonstrations and interact with the birds.

 Birds up to pheasant size are captured in mid-air, and mammals such as rabbits are taken as they attempt to flee.

 Generally a bare site on a cliff edge, in a tree or in a scrape on the ground.

TRACK N° 16

A piercing, repetitive *kek-kek-kek*, as well as high-pitched whistles and screams, especially when in flight. At the nest, birds utter soft mews.

17 | Weka

The weka was once widespread but is now confined to the eastern Bay of Plenty, north-west Nelson, the west coast of the South Island and some offshore islands. It favours open country, forest margins, rocky shores and sand dunes. The reddish-brown plumage is darker in South Island birds. Roughly the size of a hen, the weka is flightless, but swims well and possesses a strong homing instinct. When seen in the open in search of food, it constantly flicks its tail.

 Seeds, fruit, invertebrates, lizards and mice; eggs are robbed from ground-nesting birds and from petrel burrows.

 A nest of dry grasses, lined with leaves and feathers, is well hidden under logs or rocks or in thick vegetation.

TRACK N° 17

Repetitive, high-pitched *coo-wheet*, *coo-wheet* whistle, rising on the second syllable (not unlike a kiwi). Other birds nearby may join in chorus, which is often heard at dusk.

18 | Pukeko

The pukeko or purple swamphen is found throughout New Zealand in lowland swamps, damp pasture, lake edges and urban ponds, and – perilously – beside motorways. Its vivid blue-and-black plumage and stout red bill are impossible to miss as it strides across watery terrain on sprawling feet, constantly flicking up its white undertail feathers. The pukeko flies clumsily, with legs dangling, but can fly long distances and swims well. Pukeko often live in groups of related birds or form pairs.

 Eats varied plant matter and often holds long shoots in one foot, like a parrot. Also takes insects, frogs and birds' eggs.

 A deep bowl of rushes and grasses is built among clumps of rushes or sedge near water or in raupo swamps.

TRACK N° 18

Calls in raucous, high-pitched screeches, grunts, clicks or musical *tuk-tuk* calls. Ear-piercing *kweep* is an alarm and contact call.

9 | South Island Takahe

20 | Australian Coot

The takahe is the largest member of the rail family, the species having increased in size over centuries in the absence of any need to fly. The small mainland population is confined to the Murchison Mountains of Fiordland; other birds have been introduced to predator-free offshore islands and mainland sanctuaries. The related pukeko is smaller and of a lighter build (being capable of flight).

Self-introduced, the coot first made its home in New Zealand in the late 1950s and is today found throughout the country on large freshwater lakes fringed with reeds or raupo. On urban lakes it mixes with other waterfowl, but is marked out by a black plumage and white bill. Spending most of its time on the water, the bird swims well and flies strongly over long distances. In the breeding season, pairs aggressively defend their territory from other birds. At other times of the year, coots often form flocks, especially when moulting.

 Eats shoots and stems of red tussock and seeds of snow tussock. When snow covers the tussock, takahe dig for fern rhizomes in beech forest.

 Eats aquatic plants and invertebrates; also forages on marginal grasses.

 Builds a deep nest bowl of fine grasses and tussock shoots in bowers of tussock clumps, lining it with soft grasses.

 Builds a large, floating nest of reed stems, raupo and weed in reed beds or under low, trailing willow branches.

 TRACK N° **19**

Contact call sounds similar to the weka's *ee-wee* with a rising inflection; duet call is a *coo-eet coo-eet*. Alarm call is a deep *oomf*.

 TRACK N° **20**

A harsh, penetrating *kraak* as well as an explosive *kut*.

21 | Eastern Bar-tailed Godwit
Kuaka

*Godwits upon arrival (left) and before the retu
migration north (abov*

Eastern bar-tailed godwits are the most numerous of the migrant waders to arrive in New Zealand each spring, with some 100,000 birds flocking to estuaries, inlets and mudflats along both eastern and western coasts. Having flown 14,000 km from tundra regions of Alaska, the birds are lean and drab.

The godwit is conspicuous among other waders, particularly by its greater size and also its long, upcurved bill. The female is larger than the male and has a longer bill.

Bar-tailed godwits mingle with other waders on their high-tide shellbank roosts. They often sweep across the feeding grounds in massed flocks, and then jostle together again in noisy assemblies. At low tide, they spread across the mudflats and shallow pools, feeding rapidly.

By the autumn, the godwits have prepared for the return migration to their breeding grounds in the Arctic, with a noticeable build-up of body fat and old feathers moulted to reveal bright russet plumage on the face and underparts of males. Females have paler russet underparts. Birds circle in practice flights before departing, with flocks finally leaving in a V formation.

 Probes deeply into mud to dig out molluscs, crustaceans and marine worms. Also takes floating organisms under water.

 Nests in the Arctic, forming a shallow scrape on the ground among brown stubbly grasses.

TRACK N° **21**

In flight the birds utter echoing *kew-kew* and soft *kit-kit* calls, and while roosting at high tide they chatter excitedly.

2 | Pied Oystercatcher
Torea

23 | Pied Stilt
Poaka

The South Island pied oystercatcher is seen in estuaries and sheltered bays throughout New Zealand. Flocks of thousands occur on the Firth of Thames and Manukau Harbour, where they are seen feeding together or resting on shellbanks and sandspits at high tide. The bird is unmistakable, with its black-over-white plumage, scarlet legs, and bright orange bill and eyes.

Also known as the black-winged stilt, this wader occurs throughout New Zealand in freshwater wetlands, lagoons, tidal estuaries, marine mudflats and wet pastures. It is easily recognised by its pied black-and-white body, fine black bill and long, thin, pinkish-red legs, which trail well behind the tail in flight. Pied stilts have increased in numbers since European settlement and are often seen in large flocks. They are uncommon on Stewart Island and offshore islands.

 Probes in sand or mud for molluscs, marine worms and small fish. Also finds earthworms and grubs on pasture.

 Diet includes molluscs, crustaceans and tiny aquatic organisms, as well as earthworms and insects in pasture.

 Migrates to South Island to nest on shingle riverbeds, pastures and lake shores. Nest is a scrape in shingle or a shallow bowl in pasture. Twigs or shells may line or decorate it.

 Birds nest singly or in loose flocks near water, making a simple scrape lined with sticks, grasses and roots.

TRACK N° 22
Shrill, piping *kleep-kleep* and musical *tu-eep* calls with rippling *ku-vee-ku-vee-ku-vee* ending in quieter notes during courtship. Alarm call is a *pic-pic-pic*.

TRACK N° 23
The most frequently heard call is a rapid, puppy-like *yep-yep-yep*, uttered while feeding, in defense, and at night as the bird flies across land to another feeding site.

24 | New Zealand Dotterel
Tuturiwhatu

25 | Spur-winged Plover

This threatened dotterel is now mainly seen north of Hawke's Bay and Kawhia, apart from a small population on Stewart Island (which is a separate subspecies). The bird is often heard before it is seen because it is so well camouflaged on sandy beaches, its pale brown-and-white winter plumage changing to a sandy russet prior to breeding. The dotterel walks or runs rapidly, and bobs its head distinctively when pausing to feed.

The spur-winged plover or masked lapwing is about the size of a rock pigeon, with grey-brown upper parts, white underparts, black head and nape, and yellow bill and wattles. The yellow spur on the shoulder of each wing may be used defensively or in display. Now common throughout New Zealand, the plover occurs on pastures, riverbeds, lagoons, lake shores and sheltered coasts. It flies with a distinctive floppy wingbeat. Birds are often seen in pairs; flocks may form in autumn.

 Takes molluscs and crustaceans (such as sandhoppers) from sand, crabs from mud, and crickets and worms from grass.

 Crustaceans and molluscs on coast; insects and worms on pastureland.

 A scrape in the sand is often placed near driftwood or clumps of marram grass or spinifex. On Stewart Island, nests inland in low vegetation on the open tops.

 Usually a depression in pasture or on shingle, lined with a few strands of grass. In arable pasture pairs may nest on buildings.

TRACK N° 24

Calls are commonly a series of short churps, a single *prip*, reedy *trrrt* and *turr* sounds, or when disturbed, a high-pitched, explosive *pweep* or *chip*.

TRACK N° 25

Noisy, rattling and rather grating call of *kitter–kitter–kitter* or *rikka–rikka*. Utters loud staccato sounds at night.

6 | Red-billed Gull
Tarapunga

ommon throughout New Zealand, this gull, hich is so conspicuous on coasts and in ban parks, hustling picnickers for scraps, es not venture far inland except in stormy eather. The adult is easily discerned from her gulls by the bright red bill and legs and le grey back. The tail is white. The black-d-white wingtips, when folded, display a olka-dot effect, which is most noticeable hen the bird is roosting.

 Takes small fish, molluscs, crustaceans and marine worms. In urban locations, eats worms, insects and food scraps.

 Forms dense colonies on rocky islands, headlands, shellbanks and sandspits. Nest is a shallow bowl in the top of a mound of seaweed, sticks and grasses.

TRACK N° **26**

A high-pitched, strident *kraa-kraa-kraa* and *kee-aar*, and an occasional *chit-chit-ta*.

27 | Caspian Tern
Tara-nui

Found throughout the country, the Caspian tern favours shallow-water habitats on estuaries, lagoons, riverbeds and lakes, occasionally roosting with other terns and gulls. Birds breed in large loose colonies or as lone pairs, on sandspits, headlands and lake shores. This large tern is easily recognised by its large size, big red bill, black legs and black cap, which during winter may be flecked with white. The tail is forked. The Caspian tern flies strongly on sickle-shaped wings.

 Catches fish close to the shore by diving from 8–10 metres above the surface. Also feeds on eels, trout and carp at inland lakes.

 Nest is a shallow, unlined hollow scraped out in sand or shingle.

TRACK N° **27**

Calls include a harsh, raucous *karak* or *karh-kaa*, a *yakketi-yak*, and a rattling *ra-ra-ra-ra*. Repeated *kuk-kuk-kuk* sounds are made at intruders.

28 | New Zealand Pigeon
Kereru

*Feeding on nikau berries (left); male arriv
for nest duty (abov*

This magnificent fruit pigeon is resident throughout New Zealand in mixed forests, where trees produce an abundance of fruit.

The New Zealand pigeon, often incorrectly called a woodpigeon, is a large, heavy bird and tends to be clumsy when landing and as it feeds among foliage. The swaying and rustling of tree branches and the dropping of ripe fruit tend to reveal the bird's location. Its nests are vulnerable to predation by possums and ship rats.

The iridescent green head, throat and wings contrast with the pure white breast and underparts. The bird's rounded wings assist flight among forest trees, with its strong whistling wingbeats.

The kereru flies long distances in search of suitable food. Seeds from fruiting native trees pass intact into the droppings and are dispersed widely. In this way the New Zealand pigeon fulfils an important ecological role in helping to propagate the forest.

 Eats fruits, foliage, buds and flowers, including broom, clover and lucerne. Favours the large fruits of miro, tawa, taraire and puriri, being the only bird able to swallow them.

 Builds a flimsy platform of loosely crossed small twigs, usually in a substorey tree where there is plenty of overhead cover.

TRACK N° 28

Usually utters a gentle *kuu–kuu*, often when pairs are interacting.

9 | Kakapo

30 | Kaka

e world's heaviest parrot, the kakapo is ghtless, nocturnal and solitary in habit. face is flat and owl-like with a stout bill, ile the dappled green plumage blends with fern and tussock habitat. Vulnerable to edation by stoats and cats, the kakapo is tically endangered. The last wild birds from rdland and Stewart Island were moved island sanctuaries. A kakapo may live for –100 years.

Found mainly in large tracts of mature native forest, this medium-sized parrot inhabits scattered locations on the three main islands. Females are vulnerable to stoat predation at nest sites, and today the bird's strongholds are offshore islands such as Great Barrier, Little Barrier, Kapiti and Codfish. Kaka fly strongly, and island birds often visit the mainland in winter to access food. The upper wings are red-bronze and underwings orange. The brush-tipped tongue is used to take nectar when in season.

 Strips and crushes foliage, seeds and fruit, also grubbing out rhizomes and roots with its hooked bill. One foot is used to hold food to the bill.

 Female forms a nest scrape in a shallow hollow, under a tussock or in a hollow log or tree stump.

Feeds on fruit, foliage, shoots, nectar, sap and insects, as well as grubs dug from both solid and rotten wood.

Deep, dry cavities in mature forest trees are lined with wood dust.

TRACK N° 29

A courting male calls from his 'bowl' (a circle of flattened vegetation); after grunts, he calls in ever deeper echoing, booming notes. Male also utters *skrarks*, mews and a metallic *ching*.

TRACK N° 30

Close communication call is a *kra-kra-kra-kra-ah-kra-ah*. Other calls are musical whistles and warbles, interspersed with a harsh *krraaaack*.

31 | Kea

The world's largest alpine parrot, the kea lives in high-altitude forests and herbfields. Its olive-green upperparts are edged in black, like scales, and the scarlet underwing is obvious in flight. This inquisitive bird is often seen near huts or car parks, where it delights in pulling at windscreen wipers and pecking at tyres. The kea flies strongly, soaring high and playfully tumbling on air currents.

 Feeds on seeds, foliage, insects and nectar, and uses its bill to dig roots and grubs from the ground. Also rummages through rubbish for scraps.

 A nest built from sticks, grasses and lichens is lined with moss and sited under logs, near rocks or among tumbled boulders.

TRACK N° 31

A high-pitched, penetrating *kee-aaa kee-aaa kee-aaa* or *ah-ah-ah-ah-ah-ahrrrrr* and *ee-aarrrh*. Also gives whistles and soft murmurs.

32 | Eastern Rosella

Originally from Australia, the rosella has lived in New Zealand for a century or so. Common in parts of the North Island, with small numbers in the South Island, it is found in varied habitats including forest, farmland and urban areas near tree shelter. Seen in pairs or small groups, birds visit gardens in winter. The colourful plumage and long tail make recognition easy, especially when the bird is flushed from the ground and flies up into a nearby tree.

 Feeds on shoots of shrubs, thistle seed, tree fruits, flowers, nectar and insects, and also takes seeds and fallen fruit.

 Nests in dry tree cavities, hollows in broken tree limbs and trunks of tree ferns, with wood dust useful as a lining.

TRACK N° 32

Calls include the *kwink* flight call, two- or three-note whistles, and a screech when alarmed. While feeding, makes muted babbling sounds and excited, budgerigar-like chattering.

3 | Red-crowned Parakeet
Kakariki

34 | Shining Cuckoo
Pipiwharauroa

home in lowland native forest, this
rakeet is now more commonly seen on
shore islands than on the mainland, where
s open to predation by cats, stoats and
s, in part because it often feeds on the
ound. The bright green plumage and head
ped with red provide good camouflage
nong forest trees. Parakeets may be seen
ne, in pairs or groups, especially when
ey fly some distance to find food in winter.
ght is rapid and direct.

More often heard than seen, this small
cuckoo arrives in New Zealand from the
Solomon Islands in September. The shining
cuckoo is found throughout New Zealand,
inhabiting forests and open country with
shelter belts, as well as urban areas. It is well
camouflaged by shimmering green upper
wings and heavily barred underparts. Though
usually solitary in habit, birds sometimes
form small flocks in spring and summer.

 Takes caterpillars, craneflies, scale
insects, spiders and slugs from foliage.

 Feeds on flowers, buds, fruits, leaves,
nectar, fallen seeds and insects.

 Does not build its own nest, but lays
its egg in the nest of a grey warbler.
The hatched chick is fostered by the
grey warbler until it leaves the nest to
migrate to the Solomons.

 Favours tree cavities, sometimes close
to the ground, but also nests in a rock
crevice or burrow or amid vegetation.
Nest may be lined with leaves.

TRACK N° **33**

While feeding, birds sometimes engage in
continuous, rapid, staccato *ki-ki-ki-ki-ki-ki-ki*.
During flight, birds utter a repeated *ke-ke-ke*.

TRACK N° **34**

Repetitive slurred, silvery double-note
whistles increase in intensity, ending on several
downward notes. Also *tsee-ew tsee-ew* and
cheoow when several birds flock together.

35 | Morepork
Ruru

An adult brings prey (left); three-week-old owlets (abov

The morepork is widely distributed throughout forested regions of the mainland and offshore islands. Its familiar call is also heard at night in parks and suburbs. This owl's name is derived from its call, although the true sound is closer to *quor-quo*.

Quite unlike the introduced little owl, which can be seen hunting by day, this endemic bird is more darkly coloured and nocturnal in habit, with rounded wings that help it manoeuvre around forest trees.

The bird's flight is rapid and silent. As with all owls, the morepork's flight feathers are edged with a soft fringe that effectively muffles the sound of air rushing over the wings during flight. This allows the morepork to swoop silently on prey in a surprise attack.

Hearing is especially acute, partly due to the feathery facial disc that channels sound to the morepork's ears. (Experiments have shown that an owl can accurately locate the position of the sound of a moving insect eve when its eyes are masked.)

The morepork's powerful, sharp talons and strong, hooked beak are adapted for capturing and killing live prey.

 Preys on weta and other insects, small birds, mice and geckos; also snaps up moths attracted to urban street lights.

 Nests are sited in tree cavities or beneath large epiphytes and are lined with powdered wood.

TRACK N° 35

Quor-quo call is heard at night; also a continuous *quork-quork* and a short, rising *quee*. Hunting call is a *mew* sound, and a vibrating *cree-cree* is heard in the breeding season.

36 | New Zealand Kingfisher
Kotare

[Th]e kingfisher frequents forests, open country, [urb]an gardens and the coast. Birds that live [inl]and often migrate to the lowlands and [co]asts in winter. The kingfisher often perches [on] posts or power lines, watching intently [for] live prey. Being a wary bird, however, it is [ea]sily disturbed and may only be seen as a [fla]sh of bright blue as it flies off.

Captures live prey – lizards, fish, insects, mice and small birds – often without alighting, except when diving for fish. Uses strong bill to batter large prey before swallowing it whole.

Uses its bill to bore a 20 cm-long tunnel and terminal chamber in a clay bank, rotting tree trunk or tree cavity. Eggs are laid on the earth or wood chips.

TRACK N° 36

Territorial calls are an insistent and urgent kik-kik-kik-kik-kik, uttered in duet. Chicks make a buzzing soliciting call in the nest.

37 | South Island Rifleman
Titipounamu

The rifleman is New Zealand's smallest bird. It is most commonly found in beech forests in both main islands, and also occurs on some offshore islands. Green-grey and white in colour, with a short tail, this bird can be identified by the flicking of its wings, flittering flight and jerky hops through the branches. When feeding, it often spirals up from the base of a tree, poking its bill into bark crevices and foliage, then it drops and repeats the process on another tree. Pairs keep small, year-round territories.

Insects, spiders, moths and beetles, found in bark crevices and on foliage.

Nest of dry grasses, moss and twigs, lined with feathers, is built in a tree or cliff cavity or on a bank.

TRACK N° 37

Call is a rapid, high-pitched zipt–zipt–zipt–zipt, sometimes beyond the range of human hearing.

31

38 | North Island Kokako

Adult (left); female preening chicks at the nest (abo

A member of the ancient family of wattlebirds, the kokako possesses distinctive blue wattles at the base of its black bill and facial mask. The plumage is otherwise an overall grey.

The kokako is threatened by introduced predators, especially ship rats and possums, and land clearance has removed vast tracts of its preferred mixed-forest habitat. Since it is a weak flyer, the bird cannot easily move to other forest habitats. Kokako have been relocated to island sanctuaries such as Hauturu/Little Barrier, Tiritiri Matangi and Kapiti.

When feeding, the kokako holds its food in one foot, parrot fashion. It springs from branch to branch on its strong legs, using its rounded wings to maintain balance. The bird works its way up branches into the canopy, and then glides down again, before moving to another tree.

Paired birds maintain a permanent territo and may be seen mutually preening and duetting throughout the year.

 Kokako eat a wide range of flowers, foliage, fruits and some insects. Old forests are the best source of this broad diet.

 A bulky nest is built on a base of stick overlaid with ferns, lichen and moss. It usually well hidden among epiphytes in the crown of a tree fern.

TRACK N° 3

Gives powerful, resonant, organ- and flute-like notes along with mews and clucks. Pairs sing in a duet of clusters of double notes, in a haunting minor key.

9 | North Island Saddleback
Tieke

40 | Stitchbird
Hihi

ange wattles, which are larger in the ale, mark the saddleback as one of the attlebirds. It was once found in forests roughout New Zealand, but introduced edators quickly eradicated it from the ainland and it now lives only in predator-e islands and mainland sanctuaries. The umage is glossy black with a chestnut ddle and rump. Remaining in pairs year-und in a permanent territory, saddlebacks e noisy and highly active birds.

The stitchbird is found only in the North Island and, as a result of losses to introduced predators, is today further restricted to sanctuaries such as Hauturu/Little Barrier Island and Tiritiri Matangi. The male possesses a black head with ear tufts and canary-yellow shoulders, while the female is an overall moss-brown; in both sexes there is a white upperwing patch. This is an active bird, often cocking its tail while foraging or when interacting with other stitchbirds.

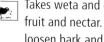 Takes weta and other insects, spiders, fruit and nectar. Uses its strong bill to loosen bark and dig in wood for insects.

 Sips nectar from flowers and takes native tree fruits as well as insects, the latter especially when rearing chicks.

 A shallow cup of twigs, bark, grasses and leaves is lined with grasses and built in a tree hollow or rock crevice.

 A cup-shaped nest of rootlets, sticks and fine grasses, lined with feathers, is built in a cavity such as a tree hole.

TRACK N° **39**

Males sing different territorial dialects, some of which sound like a squeaky wheelbarrow. A common call is a *cheet-te-te-te* chatter. Quiet calls include musical, flute-like calls.

TRACK N° **40**

Male gives a loud *ti-ora* whistle, and both sexes call with an explosive *see-si-ip*. Male also produces a subdued warbling song, which may contain mimicked calls of other species.

41 | Grey Warbler
Riroriro

Widespread in New Zealand, the grey warbler may be found in forests, scrubland and sheltered gardens, usually in pairs or family groups. What it lacks in looks – dull grey above, patchy white below – the bird makes up for with its liveliness and far-carrying song. Small and light, it can hover to pluck insects from leaves with its fine bill, and the rapid fluttering of its wings dislodges insects from the foliage.

 Insects (flies, beetles and caterpillars) and spiders; also small ripe fruits.

 A hanging, pear-shaped dome of moss, grasses, lichen and leaves, deeply lined with feathers, with a side entrance hole. Often parasitised by the shining cuckoo (see page 29).

(see page 29).

TRACK N° 41

The full song, a much-loved herald of spring, is a high-pitched, trilling and tremulous warble, often halted mid-song, and then repeated. Alarm note is a rapid twitter.

42 | Bellbird
Korimako

Named for its beautiful pealing song, the bellbird is widespread in New Zealand, foun in forest, scrubland, parks and gardens. It is rare in Northland and coastal urban Auckland. The male is bright olive-green wit a purple head, while the smaller female is dull olive-green with a pale cheek stripe. Pa bond for life and keep the same territory for years. Through nectar feeding, the bellbird helps pollinate many forest flowers.

 Sips nectar with its brush-tipped tongu and also eats fruit, insects and spiders Insects are more commonly eaten whe rearing young.

 Bowl of twigs, leaves and grasses, line with feathers and moss, is hidden in shrubs or crevices and hollows of tree

TRACK N° 42

Dawn song consists of three to five melodious, liquid, bell-like notes, and can be spectacular en masse. Female gives a distinctive musical song. Alarm call is a *chet, chet, chet, chet*

3 | Tui

ne of our best-loved songsters, the tui is
ainly a forest bird, though it is now familiar
 urban parks and gardens in many parts of
e country. It is unmistakable with its white
roat tuft and fine white plumes across
e upper back, as well as the iridescent
rquoise plumage and bronze upper parts.
ght is rapid, noisy and direct. Sometimes
e tui soars above low forest before diving
isily back again.

 Sips nectar from a variety of flowers
(thus helping to pollinate them); also
takes berries, insects and spiders.

 A bulky, twiggy-looking nest of sticks
and dried grasses is built in a tree fork
or up in the canopy.

TRACK N° **43**

Song is a cluster of quickfire snorts,
gurgles, rattles, croaks, clicks, gongs and melodic
chimes. Also utters fluid, rich and resonant trills.
Some sounds are above human hearing.

44 | Whitehead
Popokatea

The whitehead is found only in the North
Island, inhabiting native forest, pine forest
and scrubland. An active bird, it is generally
seen in family groups that move noisily about
in the upper canopy in search of food. Where
insect prey is abundant, it may be seen with
parakeets, fantails and saddlebacks. The male
has olive-brown plumage with a white head,
while the female and young are duller.

 A wide range of arthropods such as
spiders, beetles, moths and caterpillars
is gleaned from foliage and beneath
bark. Small fruits are also eaten.

 A neat, cup-shaped nest of grasses,
moss and leaves, bound together with
spider's web and lined with feathers, is
usually built in a shrub or tree fork.

TRACK N° **44**

Highly vocal, calling with a repeated,
loud *zseet-zseet-zseet* and *twe-twe-twe* as well as
musical chirps, followed by a canary-like trilling
song with a rolling *tweedle-weedle-weedle*.

45 | Yellowhead
Mohua

This South Island species has declined as a result of nest predation by stoats and ship rats. Today the yellowhead is mainly confined to the beech forests of Fiordland and Mount Aspiring National Park, with a few outlying populations near Arthur's Pass and in Southland. It is an attractive bird, with a prominent canary-yellow head and chest and olive-green upperparts; the female is slightly duller than the male. Yellowheads habitually feed in family groups in the upper canopy.

 Finds a wide range of invertebrates on foliage and under tree bark. Also takes small fruits.

 A nest of grasses, moss and leaves is bound together with spider's web and built in a tree cavity.

TRACK N° 45

Very vocal, with a loud, canary-like song of trilling notes and whistles. Also gives a rapid, staccato chatter.

46 | White-backed magpie

Introduced in the 1860s, the white-backed or Australian magpie is found across much of New Zealand, inhabiting open pasture bordered by trees. Both sexes sport the black-and-white markings, although on the female the white is flecked with grey. Birds occur in pairs throughout the year and guard their territory fiercely, even attacking dogs or people who stray too close. The magpie is now considered a pest as it preys on the eggs and nestlings of other birds.

 Insects, spiders, lizards, mice, nestlings and eggs; grain, seedlings and carrion.

 A bulky structure of sticks, grasses and pine needles, lined with sheep's wool and grasses, is built high in a tall tree.

TRACK N° 46

Utters a 'glorious carol' of warbling, flute-like notes, particularly in the morning when going to roost (described by poet Denis Glover as 'quardle oodle ardle wardle doodle').

47 | Fantail
Piwakawaka

The fantail is widespread in New Zealand, occurring in almost any habitat where insects may be found. The plumage appears in two forms, with pied birds in the north and both pied and black birds in the south. Active and vocal, the fantail constantly flicks its black-and-white tail feathers into a fan, whether during flight, feeding or display. Pairs are territorial most of the year, but form loose winter flocks that feed in forest clearings.

 Forages in forest litter or sweeps its tail across foliage to dislodge insects. Flying prey is caught mid-air.

 Cup of grasses, moss and lichen, bound with spider's web and lined with feathers, is woven across a branch, often with a dangling tail of material.

TRACK N° 47

Song is a high–pitched, penetrating *cheat cheat cheat*, sometimes with a series of spluttering squeaks. Alarm call is a single loud *cheat*.

48 | Tomtit
Miromiro

The tomtit is distributed throughout New Zealand, occurring in forest and tall scrub, with beech forest a favoured habitat. Pairs usually keep together all year, maintaining a large territory. The male's head and upperparts are mainly black with underparts white (though these are yellow-tinged in the South Island), and the female is brown with a white breast. The male is more inquisitive than the female, so is more likely to be seen.

 Insects, including beetles, wasps, flies and moths; worms; small fruit.

 A cup-shaped nest formed from moss, bark fragments and rootlets, bound with spider's web and lined with feathers, is hidden in a tree hole or cleft, or in a cavity in a bank.

TRACK N° 48

Contact call is a high–pitched *see-seee* or a thin whistle. Male also sings with warbling *yodi-yodi-yodi* notes.

49 | New Zealand Robin
Toutouwai

50 | Skylark

Robins are patchily distributed across New Zealand in native and exotic forests, where pairs occupy territories all year. The upperparts are a blackish grey, and the belly shows a patch of white (tinged yellow in South Island robins). Noticeable features include the long black legs, shiny black eyes and perky attitude. Birds may be seen perched near forest tracks, watching for insects, or hopping on the forest floor, though here they are vulnerable to stoats and cats.

The skylark was introduced from Europe in the 1860s and is now common throughout New Zealand in open country, on sand dunes and high in subalpine herbfields. With its modest brown upper wings, buff underparts and small crest, the bird is usually identified by the sound of the male's soaring, rippling song. Skylarks are very wary of predators when nesting, and may attempt to hide the nest's location by alighting a short distance away and run the final stretch under cover.

 Insects (including large prey such as weta and stick insects), spiders, worms.

 Takes seeds from a variety of plants, as well as insects and grubs, especially when feeding chicks.

 A bulky nest of twigs, moss and rootlets, bound with spider's web and lined with tree fern scales, is built in a fork or shallow cavity in a tree.

 Nest is a cup of fine grasses in a depression on the ground, often concealed by overhanging grass tufts.

TRACK N° **49**

Territorial song is a loud, clear
chirp-chirp-chirp churp-churp chip-chip-chip
repeated, varying in pitch and increasing in
volume and tempo.

TRACK N° **50**

Song is a torrent of trills and runs,
sustained sometimes for up to five minutes and
delivered as the bird soars steeply or while poised
at a height, or as it drops towards the ground.

1 | Fernbird
Matata

52 | Silvereye
Tauhou

Salt marshes, reed swamps, flax fields and pine bogs throughout New Zealand are home to the fernbird. A sparrow-sized bird, with black- and brown-streaked plumage and a long, wispy fern-like tail, it is more often heard than seen, generally staying hidden among dense vegetation. It tends to run rather than fly, and when it does take to the air it usually keeps low and flutters only a short distance.

Self-introduced from Australia in the 1850s, the silvereye is now found throughout New Zealand in forests, scrub, orchards and gardens. This bird is also known as a white-eye or wax-eye, due to the white feathers encircling its eye. The moss-green and grey upperparts with pale tan and white underparts merge with the foliage as the bird flits rapidly from tree to tree. Flocks form in autumn and winter, but break down in spring as pairs take up breeding territories.

 Scurries among foliage and clings to the stems of flax and rushes in search of insects and spiders.

 Insects, nectar, fruits from native trees and weeds, orchard fruits.

 A nest of loosely woven dried grasses, lined with feathers, is built just above the ground among rushes or sedge, and is well concealed from view.

 A flimsy cradle of fine grasses, hairs and moss is bound with spider's web, lined with tiny leaves and hung among the outer branches of shrubs and trees.

TRACK N° **51**

Pairs keep in touch with clicking *u–plick* calls (the male utters *u* and his mate replies *plick*). Male also calls in a musical *too–lit*, with a rising second note. The alarm call is a rapid *di–di–di–di*.

TRACK N° **52**

Flock call, especially in flight, is a chirping *cli–cli–cli*, with another flock call being a plaintive *cree*. Male sings a subdued warbling song in the breeding season.

53 | Welcome Swallow

54 | Blackbird

Self-introduced from Australia, the swallow is now found throughout New Zealand, usually appearing in wetlands and on the seashore, where groups may perch on posts or power lines. The plumage may seem generally dark, but a closer look reveals indigo upper wings, buff underparts and a gleaming chestnut face and neck. The slender body, long pointed wings and forked tail are useful identifiers in flight, which is swift, swooping and sometimes soaring in pursuit of prey.

Introduced in the 1860s–70s, this mellifluous songster is now one of our most common birds, occurring in gardens and pastureland as well as native forest and alpine herbfields. The male epitomises a blackbird as we expect to see it, with its jet-black plumage and vivid orange bill, whereas the female's plumage and bill are brown. Blackbirds are territorial when breeding, but may form flocks near abundant food sources in the autumn.

 Broad diet of insects, beetles, worms and grubs, as well as berries from native trees, shrubs and orchard fruit.

 Catches flying insects, often just above water; on beaches, takes kelp flies.

 A cup of mud, reinforced with grasses and lined with feathers, is attached to a wall, a culvert, under a bridge or in a hollow tree or a sea cave.

 A bulky nest of twigs, moss and leaves, lined with grasses and bound together with mud, is built usually in hedges and trees, but sometimes on buildings.

 TRACK N° 53

Contact call is a high-pitched *zwitt zwitt* or a mix of high-pitched warbles, chattering and trills.

 TRACK N° 54

Male's song, heard from late July on, is a clear, flute-like whistle and a stream of mellow ripples interspersed with clucks. Alarm call is a *tchook* and a persistent *tchink, tchink, tchink.*

5 | Song Thrush

56 | Starling

troduced in the 1860s, the song thrush
widespread in New Zealand, occupying
rdens, parks, scrubland, and exotic and
tive forests. The upper wings are a uniform
own, and the underparts are pale buff with
ld brown spots. Usually alert and upright
bearing, the song thrush moves across the
ound in a series of runs, pauses and little
pping jumps in its search for food.

Common throughout the country, the starling
is frequently seen in pastureland and towns.
In summer, it is glossy black with a purple
and greenish sheen and yellow bill. In winter
the bill is black and feathers are white-tipped,
creating a 'starlit' effect. These sociable birds
may be seen in large flocks, especially when
feeding or when gathering in a tree to roost
at night, at which time they produce an
excited clamour that fades to a soft hum.

 Eats insects, spiders, worms and snails,
extracting the latter by picking up shells
and hammering them against a rock or
hard surface. Also takes some fruit.

 A wide range of insects, grubs and
worms, found mostly on the ground, as
well as fruits and nectar.

 A tidy nest composed of fine grasses
and moss, and smoothly lined with mud
and rotted wood, is concealed in thick
shrubbery or a tree fork.

 A loose nest of dried grasses, leaves and
twigs, lined with fine grasses, is built in
cliff crevices, tree holes and buildings.
Readily uses nest boxes.

TRACK N° **55**

Song, heard from April on, is a stream
of three rising and two falling notes: *chitty-choo
chitty-choo, oo-ee oo-ee*. Alarm call is a short
chuk or *chip*; flight call is a thin, high *seep*.

TRACK N° **56**

Characteristic call is a long, descending
chee-oo whistle. Song is a lively ramble of throaty
warbles, clicks and gurgles, interspersed with
musical whistles and mimicry of other birds' calls.

57 | Common Myna

58 | House Sparrow

Introduced from Asia in the 1870s, the common or Indian myna prefers the warmer northern half of the North Island and is often found near human habitation in noisy, small to medium-sized flocks. Commonly feeding on the ground, it may be seen foraging on roadsides, where it walks with a bold strut. The plumage is an overall brown with glossy black head and yellow face, bill and legs. White wing patches are shown in flight.

The ubiquitous sparrow is common wherever it finds food, and is often seen in flocks at human settlements and farm outbuildings. The male's plumage is brown streaked with black above and a greyish white below, with a prominent black bib and grey crown. The paler female is dull brown above and greyish white below. A white wing bar is revealed in flight, which is rapid and direct with fast flapping. Birds often feed in small flocks, which rapidly scatter if disturbed.

 Eats insects and grubs, worms, fruit and nectar.

 A bulky nest of sticks, grasses, leaves, and paper or plastic scraps is built in a a tree hole or cliff cavity or in a niche on a building. The myna sometimes evicts starlings or kingfishers from their nests.

 Eats seeds, grains and bread scraps, flower buds and fruit; also insects, especially when feeding chicks.

 A bulky dome of grasses, lined with feathers, is usually sited in a tall tree or a cavity on a building or cliff face.

TRACK N° 57
Calls are a medley of notes that are raucous, gurgling, chattering and bell-like in rapid sequence. Adults with young utter a harsh squawk. Roosting birds call in a jumble of excitable sounds.

TRACK N° 58
Calls mainly feature a monotonous chirruping and brief chirps that sometimes break into ripples or short whistles. Groups of males may produce a rhythmical chorus effect.

9 | New Zealand Pipit
Pihoihoi

e pipit has a widespread but local
stribution, favouring rough pasture and
ssockland from sea level to the high
untry, and may be seen near roadsides. It
easily confused with the skylark, although
lacks the skylark's crest. Behaviour is
e easiest guide to identification: while
e skylark spends much of its time in the
r, the pipit keeps more to the ground,
petitively flicking its tail as it walks or runs,
casionally rising in short, fluttering flights.

 Forages mostly on the ground for
insects, spiders and seeds.

 Ground-sited nest is a deep cup of
woven grass hidden beneath tussock,
bracken or tall grasses.

TRACK N° **59**

Often sings from high perches, calling in
a slightly rasping *zuit* or *cheet*, or a high-pitched,
shrill *scree* and *pee-pit*.

60 | Chaffinch

Introduced to New Zealand in 1862, the
chaffinch has adapted to various habitats,
including remote forest areas, but is most
readily seen in gardens and open country. In
both sexes a white wing bar is easily seen
in flight. The male (pictured) sports rusty
pink underparts, while the female is a duller
brown overall. Pairs are territorial during the
breeding season, but in winter chaffinches
often flock with other finches and sparrows.

 Seeds and grains as well as insects and
some fruit.

 A neat cup of dry grasses, moss and
lichen fragments, bound with spider's
web and lined with feathers, is built
in a shrub or tree fork, where it is well
camouflaged from view.

TRACK N° **60**

Normal call is a metallic *chwink* or
pink. Flight note is a *tsip*. Song, heard from late
July, is a loud, falling rattle with a final flourish:
chip-chip-pell-pell-cheery erry erry tissi cheweeo.

43

REFERENCES

Falla, RA, RB Sibson and EG Turbott, *The New Guide to the Birds of New Zealand and Outlying Islands* (revised and extended edition). London: Collins, 1979.

Gill, BJ, et al., *Checklist of the Birds of New Zealand, Norfolk and Macquarie Islands, and the Ross Dependency, Antarctica* (fourth edition). Wellington: Te Papa Press (in association with the Ornithological Society of New Zealand Inc.), 2010.

Heather, Barrie, and Hugh Robertson, *Field Guide to the Birds of New Zealand* (revised edition). Auckland: Penguin Books, 2005.

Moon, Geoff, *The Reed Field Guide to New Zealand Birds*. Auckland: Reed Books, 2004.

FURTHER READING

Davis, Lloyd Spencer, and Rod Morris, *Penguins of New Zealand*. Auckland: New Holland Publishers, 2009.

Ell, Gordon, *Attracting Birds and Other Wildlife to Your Garden in New Zealand*. Auckland: New Holland Publishers, 2009.

Moon, Geoff, *A Photographic Guide to Birds of New Zealand*. Auckland: New Holland Publishers, 2002.

Moon, Geoff, *New Zealand Wetland Birds and their World*. Auckland: New Holland Publishers, 2009.

Moon, Geoff, *New Zealand Forest Birds and their World*. Auckland: New Holland Publishers, 2010.

Moon, Lynnette, *Know Your New Zealand Birds*. Auckland: New Holland Publishers, 2006.

Ombler, Kathy, *Where to Watch Birds in New Zealand*. Auckland: New Holland Publishers, 2007.

Parkinson, Brian, *Field Guide to New Zealand Seabirds*. Auckland: New Holland Publishers, 2000.

FOR YOUNGER READERS:
Gunson, Dave, *All About New Zealand Birds*. Auckland: New Holland Publishers, 2008.

INDEX OF SPECIES

Common name	Scientific name	Status (Endemic, Native, Introduced)	Page	Track
pipit, New Zealand	*Anthus novaeseelandiae novaeseelandiae*	N	43	59
plover, spur-winged	*Vanellus miles novaehollandiae*	N	24	25
pukeko	*Porphyrio melanotus melanotus*	N	20	18
rifleman, South Island	*Acanthisitta chloris chloris*	E	31	37
robin, New Zealand	*Petroica australis*	E	38	49
rosella, eastern	*Platycercus eximius*	I	28	32
saddleback, North Island	*Philesturnus rufusater*	E	33	39
scaup, New Zealand	*Aythya novaeseelandiae*	E	14	7
shag, pied	*Phalacrocorax varius varius*	N	17	12
shelduck, paradise	*Tadorna variegata*	E	12	3
silvereye	*Zosterops lateralis*	N	39	52
skylark	*Alauda arvensis*	I	38	50
sparrow, house	*Passer domesticus domesticus*	I	42	58
starling	*Sturnus vulgaris vulgaris*	I	41	56
stilt, pied	*Himantopus himantopus leucocephalis*	N	23	23
stitchbird	*Notiomystis cincta*	E	33	40
swallow, welcome	*Hirundo neoxena*	N	40	53
swan, black	*Cygnus atratus*	I	12	2
takahe, South Island	*Porphyrio hochstetteri*	E	21	19
teal, brown	*Anas chlorotis*	E	13	5
tern, Caspian	*Hydroprogne caspia*	N	25	27
thrush, song	*Turdus philomelos*	I	41	55
tomtit	*Petroica macrocephala*	E	37	48
tui	*Prosthemadera novaeseelandiae novaeseelandiae*	E	35	43
warbler, grey	*Gerygone igata*	E	34	41
weka	*Gallirallus australis*	E	20	17
whitehead	*Mohoua albicilla*	E	35	44
yellowhead	*Mohoua ochrocephala*	E	36	45

First published in 2011 by New Holland Publishers (NZ) Ltd
Auckland • Sydney • London • Cape Town

www.newhollandpublishers.co.nz

218 Lake Road, Northcote, Auckland 0627, New Zealand
Unit 1, 66 Gibbes Street, Chatswood, NSW 2067, Australia
The Chandlery, Unit 114, 50 Westminster Bridge Road, London, SE1 7QY, United Kingdom
Wembley Square, First Floor, Solan Road, Gardens, Cape Town 8001, South Africa

Lynnette Moon has asserted her right to be identified as the author of this work.

Publishing manager: Christine Thomson
Project management: Wooden Shed Publishing Services
Sound editing: John Kendrick and Karen Baird
Original concept based on *Birds Calls for Beginners* by Doug Newman,
    published by Struik Nature, Cape Town, 2008

National Library of New Zealand Cataloguing-in-Publication Data

New Zealand bird calls / Lynnette Moon ... [et al.].
Accompanied by CD with 60 New Zealand bird calls.
Includes bibliographical references and index.
ISBN 978-1-86966-310-0
1. Birdsongs—New Zealand. 2. Birds—New Zealand.
I. Moon, Lynnette.
598.1594—dc 22

10 9 8 7 6 5

CD recorded and mastered at Stebbing Recording Centre Ltd, Auckland
George Henare appears courtesy of the Robert Bruce Agency Ltd, Auckland
Colour reproduction by Image Centre Ltd, Auckland
Printed by Toppan Leefung Printing Ltd in China

Also from New Holland Publishers

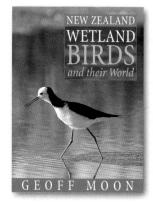

New Zealand Wetland Birds
and their World
ISBN 978 1 86966 197 7

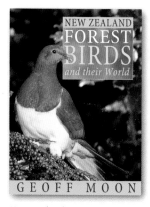

New Zealand Forest Birds
and their World
ISBN 978 1 86966 196 0

Kiwi: A natural history
ISBN 978 1 86966 292 9

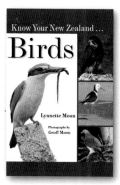

Know Your New Zealand
Birds
ISBN 978 1 86966 089 5

A Photographic Guide to
Birds of New Zealand
(2nd Edition)
ISBN 978 1 86966 327 8

Birds of New Zealand
978 1 86966 333 9